Dennis the Menace®

Prayers and Graces

by Hank Ketcham

Foreword by Ruth and Billy Graham

"For Thanksgiving" was originally printed in *Hear Our Prayer* (Garden City, N.Y.: Garden City Publishing Co.) and is copyrighted and used by permission of Fleming H. Revell (a division of Baker Book House).

"Our Daily Bread," "Bedtime," and "Always Present God" are taken from *Little Book of Prayers and Graces* (Garden City, N.Y.: Doubleday, 1952), and are used by permission of Bantam Doubleday Dell.

Book design by Frank Caruso

First edition

Published by Westminster/John Knox Press
Louisville, Kentucky

This book is printed on acid-free paper that meets the American National Standards Institute Z39.48 standard. ∞

PRINTED IN MEXICO
9 8 7 6 5 4 3 2 1

Library of Congress Cataloging-in-Publication Data

Ketcham, Hank, 1920–
    Dennis the Menace : prayers and graces / Hank Ketcham. — 1st ed.
        p.   cm.
    Summary: Traditional prayers, blessings, and table graces, paired with Dennis the Menace cartoons.
    ISBN 0-664-21993-4 (HC : acid free). — ISBN 0-664-25252-4 (PB : acid free)

    1. Children—Prayer-books and devotions—English. [1. Prayers.]
I. Title.
BV265.K483   1993
242'.62—dc20   92-17186

This booklet is dedicated to my Sunday School teachers at First Methodist Episcopal Church in Seattle, my dear grandparents, and to my Mom and Dad, who developed and encouraged our family tradition of prayers and graces — and to those others who were fooled into believing that I was a little angel.

Hank Ketcham

FOREWORD

Whoever thought Dennis the Menace would become medicine — "A merry heart doeth good like a medicine." This delightful little book will give you plenty of merriment! And the prayers and graces will bless and inspire you.

As grandparents of nineteen and great grandparents of four, we are doubly grateful to Hank Ketcham for this book and we know our children will enjoy it as well.

Ruth and Billy Graham

The joy of watching Dennis on his knees in prayer, or showing his father how he plays catch with God, restores the spontaneity and trust that faith intends.

Indeed, this book is a delightful example of how "A little child shall lead them." A glimpse of childish innocence in a theological setting is a refreshing reminder to grown-ups that prayer needn't be so secretive or complicated. As if to prove the point, dozens of simple offerings are sprinkled throughout these pages.

The honesty and confidence that Dennis has in communicating with God is contagious and I recommend it for all children and for the child in us all.

The Rt. Rev. William E. Swing, Bishop
Diocese of California

"I'm sorry, but I'm afraid I had a real innerestin' day again."

"I'M NOT SPEAKING TO YOU, DENNIS MITCHELL !"

"THANK YOU, LORD."

GOD TAKES CARE OF ME

At home or at school,
Wherever I may go,
One thought I remember
That is good to know.
It stays in my heart,
A happy little song,
That God takes care of me
The whole day long.

—*J. Lilian Vandevere*

MEAL TIME

For what we are about to receive,
O Lord, make us truly thankful.

Be present at our table, Lord;
Be here and everywhere adored.
Thy creatures bless and grant that we
May feast in paradise with thee.

—*John Wesley*

"DO YOU SAY A PRAYER BEFORE YOU EAT?"

"DON'T HAVE TO. MY MOM'S A GOOD COOK."

"I DON'T LIKE THE WAY THIS YEAR'S STARTIN' OUT!"

AT THE NEW YEAR

Thanks be to thee, Lord Jesus,
For another year to serve thee,
To love thee, and to praise thee.

A BIRTHDAY GRACE

God made the sun,
And God made the tree,
God made the mountains
And God made me.

I thank you, O God,
For the sun and the tree,
For making the mountains
And for making me.

"...AND THANK YOU FOR MAKIN' THAT BIG RAINBOW TO CELEBRATE MY BIRTHDAY!"

"THE NEXT TIME WE HAVE A THUNDERSTORM, COULD YA PUT A SMALLER BULB IN THE LIGHTNING AN' TAKE SOME OF THE *BOOM* OUT OF IT?"

DAY BREAK

Dear Lord, I offer thee this day
All I shall think, or do, or say.
For food, and all thy gifts of love,
We give Thee thanks and praise.
Look down, O Father, from above,
And bless us all our days.

FOR THOSE WE LOVE

Bless, O Lord Jesus, my parents,
And all those who love me.
Take care of me.
Make me loving to them,
Polite and obedient,
Helpful and kind. Amen.

"AND I LOVE YOU ALL THE WAY UP TO HEAVEN AND WAY PAST GOD!"

"WE'RE SINGIN' HAPPY BIRTHDAY AT OUR FROG'S FUNERAL 'CAUSE IT'S THE ONLY SONG WE ALL KNOW."

ONE EASTER

Joyfully, this Easter day,
I kneel, a little child, to pray;
Jesus, who hath conquered death,
Teach me, with my every breath,
To praise and worship thee.

—*Sharon Banigan*

FAITH

At the close of every day,
Lord, to Thee I kneel and pray.
Look upon Thy little child,
Look in love and mercy mild;
O forgive and wash away
All my naughtiness this day;
And both when I sleep and wake,
Bless me for my Savior's sake.

"GIVE ME ANOTHER CHANCE?"   "DID YOU HEAR SOME-
BODY SAY 'O.K.'?"

"IF IT'S THIS GOOD HERE, I WONDER WHAT IT'S LIKE IN **HEAVEN** ON A DAY LIKE TODAY?"

THE LOVE OF GOD

Dear God, hear me, a little child,
Who speaks to You in prayer;
Teach me today that Your great love
Is living everywhere.

FOR THANKSGIVING

For flowers so beautiful and sweet,
For friends and clothes and food to eat,
For precious hours, for work and play,
We thank Thee this Thanksgiving Day.

"OBOY! IT'S HARD TO BELIEVE HOW TIRED OF HIM WE'RE GONNA BE BY NEXT WEEK."

" WE'RE READY, LORD...LET 'ER RIP! "

COURAGE

Lord, make us ever strong and true,
For ourselves and others too.
Make us brave and keep us free,
For our country and for Thee. Amen.

CHRISTMAS

What can I give Him,
Poor as I am?
If I were a shepherd
I would bring Him a lamb;
If I were a wise man,
I would do my part;
But what can I give Him?
Give Him my heart.

—*Christina Rossetti* (adapted)

"I WONDER IF SANTA CLAUS WAS ONE OF THE THREE WISE MEN?"

"I DON'T HAVE ANY MONEY.
MYSELF IS ALL I CAN GIVE YOU."

"I MUST BE GETTIN' OLDER ... I DON'T THINK I COULD STAND CHRISTMAS OFTENER THAN ONCE A MONTH."

"I'M PLAYIN' CATCH WITH GOD. SEE? I THROW THE BALL UP.." "...AND HE THROWS IT BACK!"

COMFORT

Jesus, friend of little children,
Be a friend to me;
Take my hand and ever keep me
Close to thee.

—*Walter J. Mathans*

GOD'S PROVISIONS

God, we thank you for this food,
For rest and home and all things good;
For wind and rain and sun above,
But most of all for those we love.

—*Maryleona Frost*

"...AND BLESS THIS FOOD THAT HAS BEEN REPAIRED FOR US."

"HOW LONG BEFORE THEY START DOIN' UNTO ME WHAT I DID UNTO THEM OTHERS?"

THE LORD'S PRAYER

Our Father, who art in heaven,
Hallowed be Thy name.
Thy kingdom come,
Thy will be done, on earth
As it is in heaven.
Give us this day our daily bread,
And forgive us our debts,
As we forgive our debtors.
And lead us not into temptation,
But deliver us from evil.
For Thine is the kingdom,
And the power, and the glory,
Forever and ever. Amen.

SPRINGTIME

All things bright and beautiful
All creatures great and small,
All things wise and wonderful,
The Lord God made them all.

Each little flower that opens,
Each little bird that sings,
He made their glowing colors,
He made their tiny wings.

—*Mrs. C.F. Alexander*

"HOW CAN THINGS SO PRETTY AND CLEAN COME OUT OF *DIRT*?"

"INSTEAD OF ASKING GOD FOR SOMETHING TONIGHT, I DID SOME-THING FOR **HIM**! I TOLD HIM THE STORY OF THE THREE BEARS!"

CHARITY

May God give us grateful hearts
And keep us mindful
Of the needs of others.

IN THE MORNING

Now I wake and see the light:
'Tis God has kept me through the night.
To Him I lift my voice and pray
That He will keep me through the day.

"I LIKE IT BEST WHEN THE DAY STARTS SUNNY-SIDE UP."

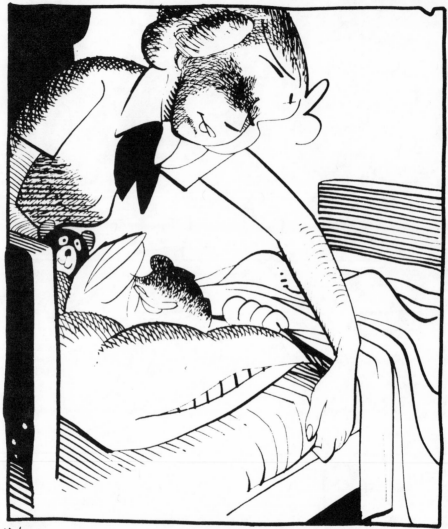

"YOU'RE LUCKY, MOM. IF YOU WERE MARGARET'S MOTHER, YOU'D HAFTA KISS *HER* GOODNIGHT!"

IN THE EVENING

Lord, keep us safe this night,
Secure from all our fears.
May angels guard us while we sleep,
Till morning light appears.

OUR DAILY BREAD

God is great and God is good,
And we thank him for our food;
By His hand we must be fed,
Give us, Lord, our daily bread. Amen.

"HOW DID GOD KNOW I WANTED YOU FOR MY MOTHER?"

"COULD YOU PLEASE MAKE HOTDOG STOP KILLIN' BIRDS? MR. WILSON'S GETTIN' TIRED OF IT, I'M GETTIN' TIRED OF IT, AN' THE BIRDS ARE REALLY GETTIN' TIRED OF IT."

BED TIME

Now I lay me down to sleep,
I pray Thee, Lord, my soul to keep;
Thy love stay with me through the night
And wake me with the morning light. Amen.

ON THE FOURTH OF JULY

Our fathers' God, to thee,
Author of liberty,
To thee we sing:
Long may our land be bright
With freedom's holy light;
Protect us by thy might,
Great God, our King.

—*Samuel F. Smith*

"I WAS JUST GONNA RING IT ONCE OR TWICE ... THEN IT STARTED RINGIN' **ME !**"

"COULD THAT BE THE ANGELS HAVING A PILLOW FIGHT?"

TOGETHERNESS

We thank Thee, Lord, for happy hearts,
For rain and sunny weather.
We thank Thee, Lord, for this our food,
And that we are together.

—Emilie Fendall Johnson

ALWAYS PRESENT GOD

God watches o'er us all the day,
At home, at school, and at our play;
And when the sun has left the skies
He watches with a million eyes.

"BEFORE I HANG UP, THANK YOU FOR THE QUARTER I FOUND TODAY. IT CAME IN REAL HANDY."

"OF COURSE I BELIEVE WHAT THE BIBLE SAYS, DEAR."

"ASK AND YE SHALL RECEIVE."

THE SHEPHERD'S CARE

The Lord my pasture shall prepare
And feed me with a shepherd's care.
His presence shall my wants supply,
And guard me with a watchful eye.

—*Joseph Addison*

The 23rd PSALM

(A song by David — and a prayer for today)

The Lord is my shepherd; I shall not want.

He maketh me to lie down in green pastures:
he leadeth me beside the still waters.

He restoreth my soul: he leadeth me in the paths of righteousness for his name's sake.

Yea, though I walk through the valley of the shadow of death, I will fear no evil: for thou art with me; thy rod and thy staff they comfort me.

Thou preparest a table before me in the presence of mine enemies: thou anointest my head with oil; my cup runneth over.

Surely goodness and mercy shall follow me all the days of my life: and I will dwell in the house of the Lord for ever.

"DON'T THEY LOOK JUST LIKE ANGELS?"